T0011081

GREAT WHITE SHARK

VS.

MEGALODON

BY CHARLES C. HOFER

CAPSTONE PRESS
a capstone imprint

Published by Capstone Press, an imprint of Capstone.
1710 Roe Crest Drive, North Mankato, Minnesota 56003
capstonepub.com

Library of Congress Cataloging-in-Publication Data
Names: Hofer, Charles, author.
Title: Great white shark vs. megalodon / by Charles C. Hofer.
Other titles: Great white shark versus megalodon
Description: North Mankato, Minnesota : Capstone Press, [2024] | Series: Beastly battles | Includes bibliographical references. | Audience: Ages 9-11 | Audience: Grades 4-6
Summary: "It's a battle between two terrifying, tooth-filled predators! The great white shark is today's largest predatory fish. But millions of years ago, megalodon ruled the seas as the ocean's deadliest hunter. Learn what makes these similar monsters of the sea so deadly. Then decide which one would triumph if they battled in the ocean's depths"— Provided by publisher.
Identifiers: LCCN 2023018987 (print) | LCCN 2023018988 (ebook) | ISBN 9781669065111 (hardcover) | ISBN 9781669065241 (paperback) | ISBN 9781669065159 (pdf) | ISBN 9781669065265 (kindle edition) | ISBN 9781669065258 (epub)
Subjects: LCSH: White shark Juvenile literature. | Carcharocles megalodon—Juvenile literature.
Classification: LCC QL638.95.L3 H64 2024 (print) | LCC QL638.95.L3 (ebook) DDC 597.3/3—dc23/eng/20230515
LC record available at https://lccn.loc.gov/2023018987
LC ebook record available at https://lccn.loc.gov/2023018988

Editorial Credits
Editor: Aaron Sautter; Designer: Bobbie Nuytten; Media Researcher: Svetlana Zhurkin; Production Specialist: Whitney Schaefer

Image Credits
Capstone: Jon Hughes, 25, 28; Dreamstime: Corey A Ford, 27; Getty Images: Alastair Pollock Photography, Cover (top), Ethan Miller, 14, Gerard Soury, 18, iStock/ARTYuSTUDIO, 27 (top), iStock/cdascher, 19, iStock/Peter_Nile, 17, iStock/USO, 9, Ken Kiefer 2, 5 (top); Shutterstock: Catmando, 21, Crudelitas, 7, EreborMountain, 13, Ewa Studio, 29, Herschel Hoffmeyer, 12, Konstantin39, 8, Mark_Kostich, 16, Noiel, 15, pim pic, 27 (background), racksuz, Cover (bottom), Rich Carey, Cover (bottom background), Sergey Uryadnikov, 11, 21, Warpaint, 5 (bottom), Willyam Bradberry, 22

All internet sites appearing in back matter were available and accurate when this book was sent to press.

TABLE OF CONTENTS

Words in **bold** are in the glossary.

SHARK ATTACK!

Are you ready for an epic battle between two terrifying sharks?

The great white shark is a deadly ocean **predator**. But long ago, the megalodon ruled the sea.

Who would win a battle between these savage sea beasts?

GREAT WHITE SHARK

MEGALODON

5

MEET THE MIGHTY MEGALODON

Megalodon was one of the biggest predators ever. Its name means "giant tooth." Scientists know this huge shark went **extinct** about 3 million years ago. But some people think a megalodon may still lurk deep in the ocean!

THE DEADLY GREAT WHITE

The great white shark is one of the ocean's largest predators. Only sperm whales and killer whales are bigger.

The great white shark spends most of its
time hunting for **prey**. It eats seals, sea lions,
and large fish.

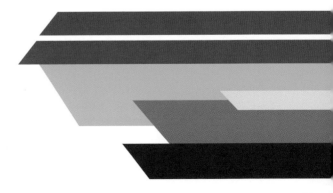

SUPER SHARK

The great white shark is one of the ocean's top predators. It's no wonder. This huge fish can grow up to 21 feet (6.4 meters) long.

This deadly shark is a mass of teeth and muscle. It can weigh up to 2,400 pounds (1,089 kilograms).

MEGA MONSTER

The great white is a big shark. But it's a shrimp compared to megalodon. This **ancient** beast grew to about 60 feet (18 m) long.

Megalodon weighed about 100,000 pounds (45,000 kg.) This giant monster could be the same size and weight as a railroad car!

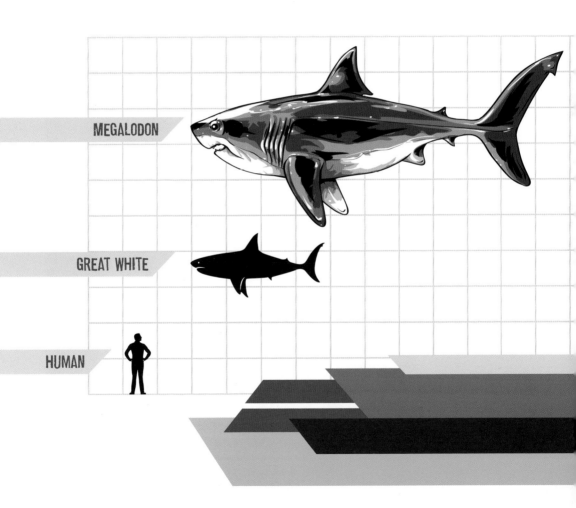

MEGALODON

GREAT WHITE

HUMAN

JAWS OF DEATH

Megalodon's jaws were up to 11 feet (3.4 m) wide. It would have no problem swallowing an adult human in one gulp!

MEGALODON JAWS

Some megalodon teeth measured 7 inches (18 centimeters) long. And it had a lot of them. This monster's mouth was filled with 276 of these huge, sharp teeth!

TEETH TIME

The great white shark has big teeth too. They are about 2.5 inches (6.4 cm) long. The shark's razor-sharp teeth are constantly being replaced. During its life, a great white shark can have as many as 20,000 teeth!

MEGALODON TOOTH = 7 INCHES (18 CM)

GREAT WHITE TOOTH = 2.5 INCHES (6.4 CM)

BUILT TO HUNT

The great white shark has a strong sense of smell. It can smell one drop of blood from a far distance. This helps the shark track down its prey.

The great white's body is built like a torpedo. It can swim up to 35 miles (56 kilometers) per hour in short bursts. That's ten times faster than the fastest human can swim.

SWIFT AND DEADLY

Megalodon probably swam along at about 11 miles (18 km) per hour. It was even faster when it attacked. Few animals could have escaped a hungry megalodon.

This giant hunter was incredibly strong too. Its bite was powerful enough to crush a car.

A MEGALODON BATTLES A GIANT OCTOPUS MILLIONS OF YEARS AGO.

DEATH FROM BELOW

The great white is a sneaky shark.
Some of its prey, like seals, stay close to
the ocean's **surface**.

The great white watches and hunts from below. With a burst of speed, the shark races to the surface. **CHOMP!** It snatches its prey with one big bite.

A GREAT WHITE SHARK CATCHES A SEAL IN ITS POWERFUL JAWS.

A MONSTER APPETITE

Megalodon might have attacked the **fins** of its prey. This **wounded** the prey so it couldn't escape. Then megalodon would move in for the kill.

To grow so big, megalodon had to eat—a lot! This giant monster could eat a whole whale in only a few bites.

TOOTHY TERRORS ATTACK!

It's time for a ferocious fish fight! The great white shark circles megalodon. It will have to be smart to beat its mighty foe.

Megalodon is a giant next to the great white. And it's hungry.

Let the battle begin!

GREAT WHITE SHARK

MEGALODON

WHO'S THE WINNER?

The great white shark is a **crafty** and sneaky killer. But megalodon has the edge in size and strength. Who will win this battle of the big sharks?

GREAT WHITE SHARK

	Great White Shark	**Megalodon**
HABITAT	coastlines in Atlantic and Pacific oceans	most oceans except Arctic and Antarctic
WEIGHT	2,400 pounds (1,089 kg)	up to 100,000 pounds (45,000 kg)
LENGTH	21 feet (6.4 m)	about 60 feet (18 m)
SPEED	35 mph (56 kph)	11 mph (18 kph)
WEAPONS	• more than 300 teeth, 2.5 inches (6.4 cm) long • jaws open 3.9 feet (1.2 m) wide • strong bite force	• about 276 teeth, 7 inches (18 cm) long • jaws open 11 feet (3.4 m) wide • massive bite force
DEFENSES	fast swimmer	huge size and strength
STRATEGY	hunts and attacks from below	attacked prey's fins

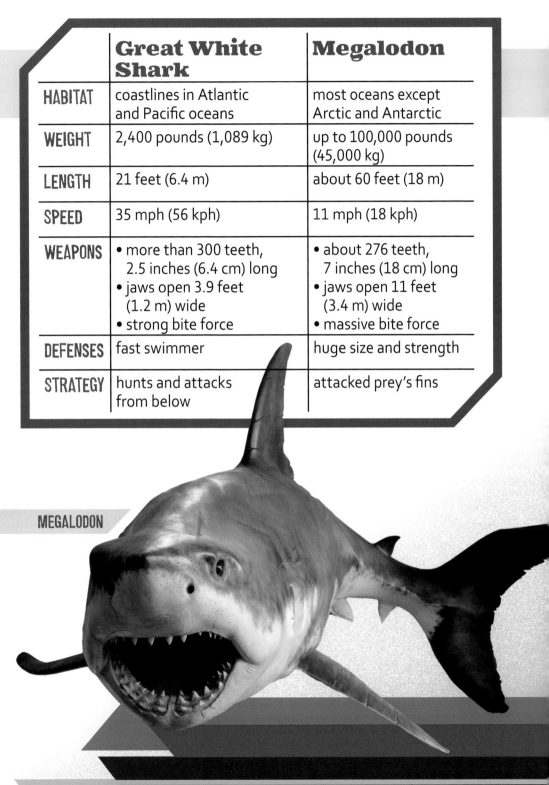

MEGALODON

GLOSSARY

ancient (AYN-shunt)—from a long time ago

crafty (KRAF-tee)—sneaky and skillful

extinct (ix-STINGKT)—no longer living; an extinct animal is one that has died out, with no more of its kind

fin (FIN)—a body part that fish use to swim and steer in water

predator (PRED-uh-tur)—an animal that hunts other animals for food

prey (PRAY)—an animal that is hunted and eaten by another animal

surface (SUR-fiss)—the outermost or top layer of something

wound (WOOND)—to cause an injury